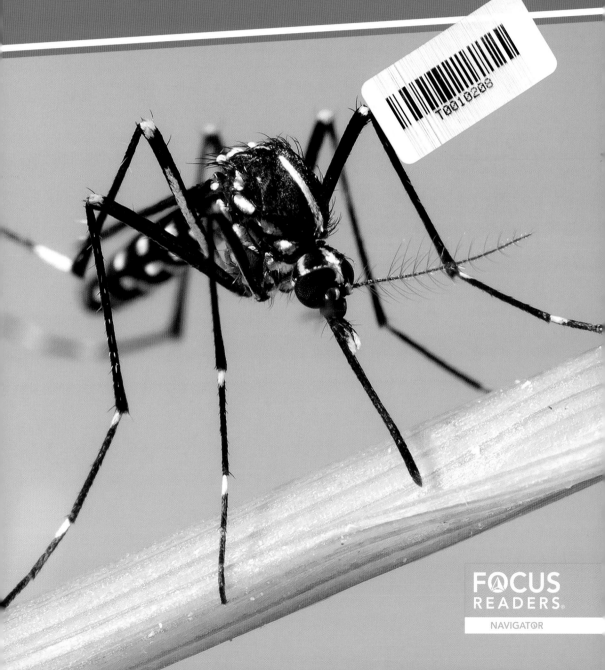

INVASIVE SPECIES
TIGER MOSQUITOES

by Emma Huddleston

FOCUS READERS

NAVIGATOR

WWW.FOCUSREADERS.COM

Focus Readers is distributed by North Star Editions:
sales@northstareditions.com | 888-417-0195

Produced for Focus Readers by Red Line Editorial.

Content Consultant: Dr. Kristen Healy, Associate Professor of Entomology at Louisiana State University

Photographs ©: Shutterstock Images, cover, 1, 4–5, 7, 15, 21, 25; James Gathany/CDC, 8–9, 11; Red Line Editorial, 13; Pascal Goetgheluck/Science Source, 16–17; iStockphoto, 19; Mohd Samsul Mohd Said/Getty Images News/Getty Images, 22–23; Roger Eritja/Alamy, 27; Carlos Mejía/El Universal/GDAPhoto/AP Images, 29

Library of Congress Cataloging-in-Publication Data
Names: Huddleston, Emma, author.
Title: Tiger mosquitoes / Emma Huddleston.
Description: Lake Elmo, MN : Focus Readers, 2022. | Series: Invasive species | Includes index. | Audience: Grades 4-6
Identifiers: LCCN 2021009203 (print) | LCCN 2021009204 (ebook) | ISBN 9781644938591 (hardcover) | ISBN 9781644939055 (paperback) | ISBN 9781644939512 (ebook) | ISBN 9781644939925 (pdf)
Subjects: LCSH: Mosquitoes--Ecology--Juvenile literature.
Classification: LCC QL536 .H87 2022 (print) | LCC QL536 (ebook) | DDC 595.77/2--dc23
LC record available at https://lccn.loc.gov/2021009203
LC ebook record available at https://lccn.loc.gov/2021009204

Printed in the United States of America
Mankato, MN
082021

ABOUT THE AUTHOR

Emma Huddleston enjoys being a children's book author. When she's not writing, she can be found reading or running outside. She lives in Minnesota with her husband.

TABLE OF CONTENTS

CHAPTER 1

ZIKA OUTBREAK

A pool of water sits in the middle of a flower. In the water, hundreds of mosquito eggs are ready to hatch. The eggs are from tiger mosquitoes. These insects can be harmful to people and animals. They carry viruses such as Zika. This virus can cause rashes and fevers. It can also cause brain problems in babies.

The center of a bromeliad can hold water. For this reason, the flower can be a breeding spot for tiger mosquitoes.

Zika virus is native to parts of Africa and Asia. Many people there have developed natural defenses against Zika. So, the virus harms few people in these areas. But in the 2000s, people likely brought mosquitoes with Zika to islands in the Pacific Ocean. People in the Pacific had not developed natural defenses against the virus. In 2007, mosquitoes caused the first known Zika **outbreak** in that part of the world.

In early 2015, Zika reached Brazil. It caused outbreaks across the country. The virus quickly spread throughout the Americas. By September 2016, people had found Zika in 60 countries. Many

Zika can cause a brain problem known as microcephaly, which makes the head smaller than usual.

babies in those areas were born with brain problems.

Luckily, the spread of Zika slowed. However, tiger mosquitoes are able to carry at least 30 other viruses besides Zika. Viruses can spread diseases. Those diseases can be especially harmful in new areas. That's why the spread of mosquitoes can be a serious problem.

CHAPTER 2

BLACK-AND-WHITE BITERS

Tiger mosquitoes are native to South Asia, East Asia, and Southeast Asia. Originally, their homes were mainly on the edges of forests. There, they bred in a variety of places. Some tiger mosquitoes laid eggs in tree holes and stumps. Others used flowers. But tiger mosquitoes can also survive in towns

Tiger mosquitoes are known for their black bodies with white stripes.

and cities. They can breed anywhere with small puddles of water.

Like all mosquitoes, tiger mosquitoes need water to survive. They live in water for three of their four life stages. Water is found in many places around people's homes. Flowerpots and birdbaths can hold pools of water. Water can also

OUT FOR BLOOD

The tiger mosquito is known for being an aggressive biter. It uses its long **proboscis** like a straw. The female mosquito pokes through skin to suck blood. At the same time, she lets out spit. The spit causes itching and swelling. Bites are also how mosquitoes spread viruses. Those viruses can lead to diseases.

Drinking blood makes part of a tiger mosquito's body look red.

collect in old tires. Mosquitoes often breed in these places.

Tiger mosquitoes tend to feed during the day. Only the female mosquitoes drink blood. The blood helps them produce eggs. Females drink blood from many animals. Given the chance, tiger mosquitoes often feed on humans.

But the mosquitoes also bite cows, squirrels, dogs, and birds. They will even bite frogs and snakes.

For much of human history, tiger mosquitoes remained in their native **habitats**. But in the 1700s, people brought tiger mosquitoes outside Asia. They spread to Hawaii. Over time, they reached other Pacific islands, too.

During the 1980s, tiger mosquitoes started to spread quickly. By 1990, people had found the mosquitoes in Europe, Africa, and the Americas. The mosquitoes often hid inside shipments. For instance, people first found tiger mosquitoes in Texas in 1985. They had traveled inside tires shipped from Japan. Later, the mosquitoes came to California from China. They had traveled in shipments of bamboo. Today, the mosquitoes live on every continent except Antarctica.

TIGER MOSQUITOES AROUND THE WORLD

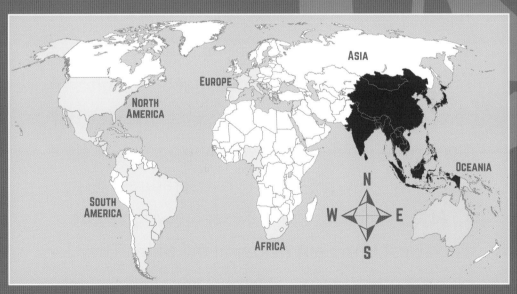

ASIA

EUROPE

NORTH
AMERICA

OCEANIA

SOUTH
AMERICA

N
W E
S

AFRICA

NATIVE RANGE   **INVASIVE RANGE**

HATCHING IN A BOTTLE CAP

Female tiger mosquitoes can lay up to 250 eggs at a time. These eggs all need water to hatch. But they don't need much. Tiger mosquitoes can hatch in the amount of water that would fill a bottle cap. Other kinds of mosquito eggs need more water to hatch.

Weather also affects tiger mosquito eggs. Eggs often hatch when they become flooded. High temperatures tend to make eggs hatch faster. But tiger mosquito eggs can wait long periods of time. Some even survive freezing temperatures.

After hatching, worm-like larvae wriggle out. Larvae eat tiny plant matter in the water. They also eat other tiny organisms. They shed their skin as they grow larger. After four **molts**, the larvae

LIFE CYCLE OF TIGER MOSQUITOES

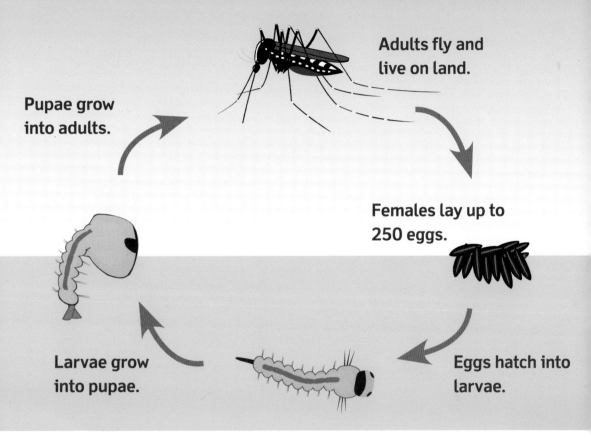

Adults fly and live on land.

Pupae grow into adults.

Females lay up to 250 eggs.

Larvae grow into pupae.

Eggs hatch into larvae.

Tiger mosquitoes do not fly far on their own. They usually stay within 1 mile (1.6 km) of where they were born.

grow into **pupae**. In a few days, the pupae become adults. Adult mosquitoes fly out of the water and live on land.

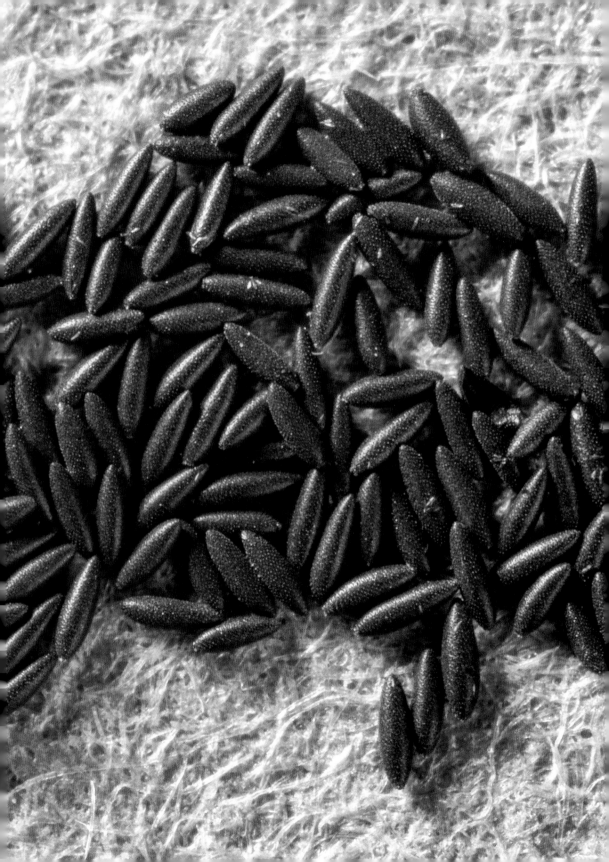

CHAPTER 3

SPREADING DISEASE

People sometimes bring a **species** to new areas. Not every species survives. But tiger mosquitoes thrive in many new places. That's partly because their eggs do not dry out easily. As a result, their eggs can still hatch after long trips. Then tiger mosquitoes begin breeding in a new place.

Tiger mosquito eggs can survive dry conditions for up to eight months.

Many kinds of mosquito eggs can withstand dry spells. These mosquitoes tend to survive well in non-native areas. But only some non-native mosquitoes become invasive. Invasive species cause major changes in native **ecosystems**. They also harm people or native species.

Tiger mosquitoes are invasive for a few reasons. First, they spread especially well in places with lots of people. In non-native cities, tiger mosquitoes face few predators. Their populations can grow large very quickly. When tiger mosquitoes take over, they are often harmful. That's mainly because they spread viruses. Those viruses can make people sick.

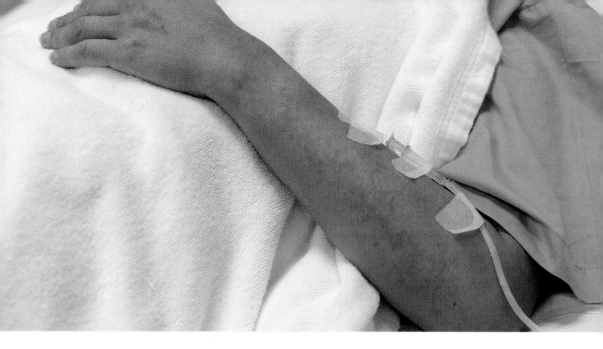

Rashes are one common symptom of diseases people can get from the viruses tiger mosquitoes carry.

Tiger mosquitoes have spread several viruses to people. Zika virus is one. A second virus is dengue. This virus often causes fevers. It leads to **symptoms** similar to the flu. In serious cases, people can die. A third virus is called chikungunya. This virus tends to cause fevers and joint pain. Yellow fever and

West Nile are two other viruses. Both can cause fevers. They can be quite serious.

The yellow fever mosquito also carries these diseases. In fact, this kind of mosquito tends to cause worse outbreaks.

HELPING HUMANS?

When tiger mosquitoes take over an area, they sometimes force other mosquitoes out. For example, the yellow fever mosquito feeds mainly on humans. It is known for spreading deadly viruses. When tiger mosquitoes force out other mosquitoes, they may help protect humans. Populations of yellow fever mosquitoes decrease. Fewer people get bitten by yellow fever mosquitoes. So, fewer people get the diseases they carry. Even so, tiger mosquitoes bring dangers of their own.

Yellow fever mosquitoes look similar to tiger mosquitoes in many ways.

But tiger mosquitoes have spread much farther around the world. They can survive in cooler regions than yellow fever mosquitoes. So, they could cause more disease overall. Plus, tiger mosquitoes can adapt over time. When that happens, they can become more dangerous.

CHAPTER 4

FINDING THE SOURCE

Scientists control tiger mosquitoes in a variety of ways. First, scientists learn as much as they can about the mosquitoes in a certain area. To do so, they often use traps. One common trap is little more than a cup of water. Female tiger mosquitoes lay eggs in the trap. People check the traps regularly for eggs.

A health worker checks traps for tiger mosquito eggs. These simple traps are known as ovitraps.

They make sure no eggs become larvae. Another trap smells similar to humans. Tiger mosquitoes are drawn to the smell. When they fly close, a fan sucks them in.

Scientists study the traps. They also study past research about tiger mosquitoes. And they may study reports about the mosquitoes from the public. Scientists compare all of this knowledge. Then they create maps. These maps show where tiger mosquitoes are most likely located. They show if the area has other mosquito species, too. Maps can also suggest how large mosquito populations are. Maps help scientists decide what control methods will work best.

A worker sprays a chemical to help control an outbreak of tiger mosquitoes.

Control methods for tiger mosquitoes often involve removing larvae. That stops tiger mosquitoes at the source. For example, people sometimes spray toxins.

Toxins are poisonous substances. Tiger mosquito larvae die after eating these chemicals. Some flies die, too. But the toxins do not harm humans. So, it is safe to spray the chemical across a large area. The spray can reach many breeding areas.

People also try to find all specific spots where tiger mosquitoes are breeding. Often, that means finding containers with water. People can throw out cans, pots, and tires. They can regularly empty birdbaths and dogs' water bowls. With fewer breeding areas, mosquito populations struggle to grow.

However, removing every breeding area is difficult. It takes lots of time and effort.

Huge numbers of tiger mosquito larvae float in a water-filled container left outside a home.

One neighborhood can have tens of thousands of breeding areas. This method also requires many people to participate. So, scientists teach communities about tiger mosquitoes. They explain how to find breeding areas around the home.

Efforts often work better when more people are involved.

A single control method rarely works by itself. As a result, people tend to use multiple methods at the same time. Scientists have found that combining approaches works best. It can help slow

SUCCESS IN NEW JERSEY

In 2009, scientists worked to lower tiger mosquito populations in New Jersey. They made education a huge part of the project. Scientists taught adults and children about tiger mosquitoes. People cleaned or removed nearly 20,000 breeding containers. Workers sprayed a toxin to kill larvae. They used other chemicals to remove adult mosquitoes. In one city, tiger mosquito numbers dropped by 75 percent.

A scientist in Mexico studies a new way to control tiger mosquitoes.

the spread of diseases. Tiger mosquitoes remain very tough to control. But scientists continue to study new ways to manage them.

FOCUS ON
TIGER MOSQUITOES

Write your answers on a separate piece of paper.

1. Write a paragraph that describes the life stages of tiger mosquitoes.

2. Are there breeding spots for tiger mosquitoes where you live? What could you do to make mosquitoes less likely to breed there?

3. The shipment of what object helped spread tiger mosquitoes around the world?
   - **A.** tires
   - **B.** bug spray
   - **C.** bottle caps

4. What is one reason that tiger mosquitoes are invasive?
   - **A.** Tiger mosquitoes tend to avoid biting people.
   - **B.** Tiger mosquitoes can harm people by spreading viruses.
   - **C.** Tiger mosquitoes usually face many predators in new places.

Answer key on page 32.

GLOSSARY

ecosystems
Communities of living things and how they interact with their surrounding environments.

habitats
The types of places where plants or animals normally grow or live.

molts
Losses of outer skeleton layers so new ones can grow in their place.

outbreak
A time when many people get sick with the same disease.

proboscis
In insects, a long body part that helps suck up and take in liquid.

pupae
Stages of life for certain insects that happen when they change from larvae to adults.

species
A group of animals or plants that are alike and can breed with one another.

symptoms
Signs of an illness or disease.

TO LEARN MORE

BOOKS

Amstutz, Lisa J. *Invasive Species*. Minneapolis: Abdo Publishing, 2018.

Hyde, Natalie. *Unusual Animal Journeys*. New York: Crabtree Publishing, 2019.

Stiefel, Chana. *Animal Zombies!: And Other Bloodsucking Beasts, Creepy Creatures, and Real-Life Monsters*. Washington, DC: National Geographic, 2018.

NOTE TO EDUCATORS

Visit **www.focusreaders.com** to find lesson plans, activities, links, and other resources related to this title.

INDEX